A Walking History of
Bellevue Avenue

николай NEWPORT,

RHODE ISLAND

THE BELLEVUE AVENUE HISTORY TRAIL

*The Bellevue Avenue History Trail,
a series of eleven markers that detail the breadth,
diversity, and preservation of Bellevue Avenue buildings,
extends from the Newport Casino to Rough Point.
Each of the eleven markers contains photographs and
text describing the history of the existing
buildings on the block as well as
buildings that no longer exist.*

*By following the markers, visitors walking
along Bellevue Avenue get a complete overview
of the architectural history and remarkable
preservation of one of America's
most legendary streets.*

*This book encapsulates the information from
all eleven markers so the landmarks and stories of
Bellevue Avenue may be enjoyed by the visitor
and armchair traveler alike.*

A Walking History of Bellevue Avenue

Newport, Rhode Island

Text by John R. Tschirch
Afterword by Ronald Lee Fleming, FAICP

*Research and editing by Holly Collins,
Caitlin Emery, and Rebecca Kelly*

Commonwealth Editions
an imprint of Applewood Books
Carlisle, Massachusetts

WALKING HISTORY OF *AMERICA SERIES*

Copyright © 2012 Applewood Books, Inc.

Published in cooperation with
The Preservation Society of Newport County

ISBN 978-1-938700-00-2

Published by Commonwealth Editions
an imprint of Applewood Books
Carlisle, Massachusetts 01741
www.commonwealtheditions.com

Commonwealth Editions publishes books about the history,
traditions, and beauty of places in New England and
throughout America for adults and children.

To request a free copy of our current print catalog
featuring our best-selling books, write to:
Applewood Books
P.O. Box 27
Carlisle, MA 01741

Book design by Barbara DaSilva

Manufactured in the United States of America

Ronald Lee Fleming, FAICP, first suggested the idea of a historic marker trail system along Bellevue Avenue when he was a trustee of The Preservation Society of Newport County. As a planner and designer, he had developed marker programs for Bicentennial projects in Boston and Lexington; in 2002, he personally provided the funding for a marker program in Newport. Working with John Tschirch, he assisted in content development, research, and editing the text for the markers that now line Bellevue Avenue. He was among the first to see the possibilities for creating this book from that material. We remain grateful for his support.

BELLEVUE AVENUE: A PRESERVATION HISTORY

John R. Tschirch
Architectural Historian
The Preservation Society of Newport County

The Bellevue Avenue National Historic Landmark District is one of the architectural treasures of the United States. This book is dedicated to telling the remarkable stories of preservation, and sometimes loss, of historic buildings on one of America's most famous streets. These stories are enlivened through the use of period photographs, newspaper accounts, and letters. Home to some of the finest nineteenth-and early-twentieth-century buildings in American architectural history, Bellevue Avenue is a place where critics have mused on and debated the meaning of the house in our national identity. It is also a case study in successful community preservation efforts. The Preservation Society of Newport County owns and maintains seven buildings and a park on Bellevue Avenue and has been instrumental in preserving the character of this legendary thoroughfare.

In the 1800s, Bellevue Avenue was nothing more than a simple dirt road. Laid out and named in 1852, it quickly became one of the most stylish streets in America. In the years between 1840 and 1914, Newport became the country's premier summer resort. The rich, powerful, and famous made Bellevue Avenue the spotlight for society, sport, and fashion. Presidents, admirals, industrial titans, writers, sportsmen, and celebrated beauties came here to promenade. Architects, decorators, and landscape designers attained celebrity status for their work on Newport's cottages. The place became a veritable laboratory of architecture by the nation's leading designers during this building boom. Every major style of house lined the avenue: Gothic Revival, Italianate, Second Empire, Stick and Shingle, Colonial Revival, and Beaux-Arts classicism.

As early as the 1850s, the newly emerging architectural press viewed Newport as an important place to look to for the most advanced ideas on domestic architecture. The nationally renowned landscape and architectural theorist and critic Andrew Jackson Downing featured the Edward King House (1845), by architect Richard Upjohn, in *The Architecture of Country Houses* (1852). This best-selling book recognized Newport's national significance as a center for architectural creativity. As the years progressed, more writers and cultural observers cast their eye on Newport. The eminent critic Marianna Griswold van Rensselaer gave the city good reviews in her article "American Country Dwellings," which appeared in *The Century Magazine* of May 1886:

> "But to the student of domestic architecture, Newport is the most interesting of our summer colonies. Its' [sic] history is the longest...Colonial houses are abundant... Its' newer portions show a characteristic instance of that way of village planning which I have already spoken of as peculiarly American—wide streets of detached houses, each with its own small lawn and garden, and all overshadowed by thickset and lofty trees. Here the architecture includes every post-colonial type: the plain, square piazzaed box; the 'vernacular' villa with 'French roof' and jig-saw fringing and abnormal hues of paint; the pseudo 'Queen Anne' cottage."

Newport possessed a variety of house types and styles, and the architectural press assured that the public would read about and see what was built in the city. Critics debated the merits of each new house, and Newport loomed large in dialogues about American art and cultural life. During the Gilded Age, the period of rapid economic growth in the years between the Civil War and World War I,

Newport became distinguished by even more lavish construction by the nation's industrialists and financiers. By 1900, dialogue about Newport centered on the increasing wealth and power of the country in general and its reflection in palatial summer houses. Hartley Davis wrote in "Magnificent Newport" for *Munsey's Magazine* in July 1900:

> "Nowhere in the world are there such beautiful summer cottages as are buil(t) in Newport. To call them cottages is an affectation. They are palaces...Newport's peculiar position rests upon an exclusiveness whose foundation is riches. The splendor of the cottages, the brilliance of the social functions, and the struggles of the ambitious to get into society, exemplify this condition of affairs...Everything in Newport is measured by the scale of millions. Even the flowers preach the gospel of wealth. Nature made it the most beautiful summer resort in the world; man has made it a monument to his colossal vanity. But it has the merit of being a beautiful and magnificent monument."

The writer Henry James lived in Newport in his youth and revisited in the early 1900s after a long absence. He remembered a simpler city of wooden houses and picturesque scenery and found, upon his return, a palatial city with classically inspired houses modeled after European palaces. James published his thoughts on Newport in *The American Scene* (1907), writing:

> "Newport, on my finding myself back there, threatened me sharply, quite at first, with that predicament at which I have glanced in another connection or two—the felt condition of having known it too well and loved it too much for the description or definition...The place itself...was more than ever, to the fancy, like some dim, simplified ghost of a small Greek island, where the clear walls of some pillared portico or pavilion, perched afar, looked like those of temples of the gods...What an idea, to have seen this miniature spot of earth, where the sea nymphs on the curved sands...might

have chanted back at the shepherds, as a mere breeding ground for white elephants! They look queer and conscious and lumpish…while their averted owners, roused from a witless dream, wonder what in the world is to be done with them. The answer to which, I think, can only be that there is absolutely nothing to be done; nothing but to let them stand there always, vast and blank, for reminder to those concerned of the prohibited degrees of witlessness, and of the peculiarly awkward vengeances of affronted proportion and discretion."

Henry James was prophetic in 1907, for many of the great houses of Newport could not be maintained into the twentieth century as private residences. The graduated personal income tax of 1913 and reforming social conditions after World War I, such as women's right to vote, forever transformed the society, culture, and finances required to maintain the life of the great house. The 1920s and 1930s proved to be two decades of extended golden summers for Newport. Houses continued to be built, but change was in the air. In the years following World War II, neglect and demolition threatened the houses of Bellevue as new tastes and economic conditions made these buildings appear as relics of a bygone era. *Life* magazine captured the state of the city in a 1944 article entitled "Life Visits a Fading Newport" with an opening essay stating:

"With a whimsy found only among the very rich, the great houses…were called "cottages" when they were built near the turn of the century. Surrounded by acres of gardens and grounds, they stand in stately rows along Bellevue Avenue in Newport, RI, which was once 'the richest street in the world.' Since the passing of the Gilded Age that these houses symbolized, two wars, a long depression, high income and inheritance taxes and the shortage of servants have dimmed Newport's splendor. The doors of many of these villas will never be opened again. A few have passed into the city's hand for non-payment of taxes because their owners have not thought them worth redeeming."

Many prophesied doom for Newport, but the founding of The Preservation Society of Newport County in 1945 signaled hope for the reverse of the city's bleak fortunes and the loss of its significant architectural and cultural heritage. Historic houses began to be saved. However, it was a difficult battle. Kenneth Chorley, director of Colonial Williamsburg, presented a speech in Newport in 1947 entitled "Only Tomorrow," in which he outlined a plan for preserving the city. Mr. Chorley proposed that great houses, such as the Vanderbilt family summer house, The Breakers (1895), be opened to the public to raise funds for the restoration of the colonial areas of Newport.

Although it is one of the most historically intact communities in the U.S., Newport suffered partly from the rise of modernism in architecture and city planning. In the period between 1945 and 1965, many in Newport and elsewhere viewed Victorian cottages and Gilded Age villas as ostentatious relics of a socially and culturally discredited past. Modern architectural tastes, in general, turned against the town's historic architecture. Two shopping centers replaced Victorian buildings and their landscapes on Bellevue Avenue in 1957 and 1958. They are adjacent to Kingscote (1841), a Gothic Revival-style landmark, and the Newport Casino (1881), a Shingle-Style masterpiece. As such, these commercial developments in mid-century Modern style radically changed the atmosphere of this section of Bellevue Avenue. One of the most important moments in the preservation of Bellevue Avenue was the threatened demolition of The Elms (1901) for development in 1961. The contents of this great Gilded Age estate were sold at one of Newport's most famous auctions. Although the art treasures were lost, the battle cry to save The Elms had been heard and the Preservation Society acquired the estate in 1962, preserving the house and its eleven acres of historic grounds, which sit at the heart of the Bellevue Avenue district.

The work of saving historic houses in Newport had an influence beyond the city's borders. Jacqueline Kennedy, upon receipt of the Preservation

Society's Antiquarian Award for her restoration work at the White House, sent a telegram in October 1962 to the Preservation Society stating:

> I have grown up seeing the wonderful things accomplished by this organization [the Preservation Society]. So I am sure it is your work in great part that made me become so interested in the restoration and preservation of our national shrines.

Although The Elms was saved, several demolitions still threatened Bellevue Avenue and prompted the Preservation Society and others to advocate for the creation of a historic district ordinance to protect Newport's treasures. The City of Newport established the Historic District in 1965. The National Park Service gave further recognition by designating the area as the Bellevue Avenue National Historic Landmark District in 1976. Today, the avenue maintains its historic residential character, but buildings represent a mixed use of private residences, adaptive reuse as educational and non-profit preservation organization offices, and condominiums.

Today, the Historic District Commission oversees the alteration of historic buildings and new construction in Newport, but preservation requires constant vigilance on the part of private citizens. The preservation of Bellevue Avenue began as a private endeavor undertaken by private citizens as a community effort to maintain the historic integrity of Newport's buildings. Today we must remain committed to preserving this heritage, recognizing the important contribution of these buildings to the character of the city and as significant landmarks in the nation's cultural legacy.

Table of Contents

FOREWORD *John Tschirch* PAGE 7

1
THE NEWPORT CASINO & ITS NEIGHBORS PAGE 15

2
KINGSCOTE & ITS NEIGHBORS PAGE 29

3
THE ISAAC BELL HOUSE & ITS NEIGHBORS PAGE 39

4
THE ELMS & ITS NEIGHBORS PAGE 49

5
424 BELLEVUE & ITS NEIGHBORS PAGE 61

6
CHATEAU-SUR-MER & ITS NEIGHBORS PAGE 79

7
FAIRLAWN & ITS NEIGHBORS PAGE 99

8
ROSECLIFF & ITS NEIGHBORS PAGE 115

9
MARBLE HOUSE & ITS NEIGHBORS PAGE 129

10
ROVENSKY PARK & ITS NEIGHBORS PAGE 143

11
ROUGH POINT & ITS NEIGHBORS PAGE 159

AFTERWORD *Ronald Lee Fleming* PAGE 175

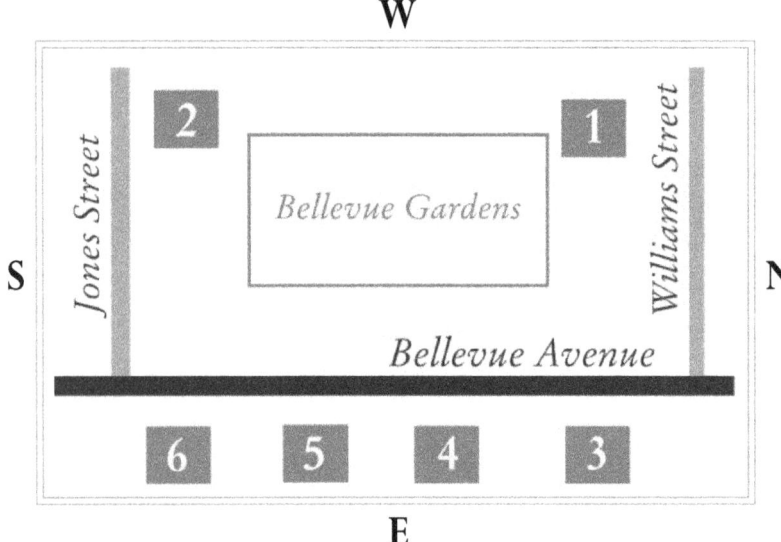

1. **Stone Villa** *(demolished)*
2. **Paran Stevens House** *(demolished)*
3. **Travers Block**
4. **Newport Casino**
5. **King Block**
6. **Audrain Building**

The Newport Casino
& Its Neighbors

THE NEWPORT CASINO and its neighbors form one of the most significant commercial blocks in the nation. This ensemble of buildings served as the gateway to fashionable Bellevue Avenue and its summer cottages. The architects of these buildings, including Richard Morris Hunt; McKim, Mead & White; and Bruce Price produced a series of picturesque stick, shingle, and brick structures that became national models for future commercial and club buildings. The centerpiece of the street is the Newport Casino, celebrated as a great American design achievement by the legendary architectural critic Marianna Griswold van Rensselaer. The Casino's club rooms, tennis court, theater, and stores catered to the social pastimes of Newport's summer residents. During the 1950s, the historic character of the street was radically changed with the destruction of Stone Villa and its gardens to make way for Bellevue Gardens Shopping Center. The Casino was saved by its transformation into the International Tennis Hall of Fame, while the other buildings on the block continue to function as commercial venues.

Stone Villa *(photo c. 1955)*

Stone Villa, gatepost owl

Stone Villa
(c. 1832–1835)

Architect: Alexander MacGregor

Alexander MacGregor, a Scottish mason who worked on Fort Adams (1826) in Newport, built Stone Villa for the Middleton family from Charleston, South Carolina. They lived in this Greek Revival house before the Civil War, when southerners were a prominent part of Newport summer life. James Gordon Bennett, heir to the *New York Herald* newspaper fortune, was Stone Villa's most famous owner. He bet his friend, Captain Candy, to ride his horse through the Newport Reading Room. After the Reading Room barred Captain Candy from its premises, Bennett declared he would build a better club. Bennett commissioned McKim, Mead & White to design the Newport Casino, which admitted women, directly across Bellevue Avenue. Stone Villa was demolished in 1957 to make way for Bellevue Gardens Shopping Center.

18 BELLEVUE AVENUE • NEWPORT

Paran Stevens House *(photo c. 1890)*

2
Paran Stevens House (c. 1866)

Architect: George Platt

Paran Stevens, known as the "Napoleon of hotel keepers," built this Second Empire style villa. A New Hampshire native and self-made man, Mr. Stevens amassed one of America's greatest fortunes in the hotel industry. Mrs. Stevens, a leading Newport socialite, once said of society, "Odd isn't it, how hard we work to get into a world which isn't after all very amusing?" The Stevens' daughter Minnie married into the English aristocracy as Lady Paget and socialized with the Prince of Wales's set. The house was demolished around 1925.

> "The cost of erecting and furnishing a villa that would be thought in any sense elegant, including the ground and the laying out, is from $50,000 to $200,000."
>
> "The Queen of Aquidneck," *Harper's New Monthly Magazine*, August 1874

20 BELLEVUE AVENUE • NEWPORT

Travers Block *(photo c. 1890)*

3
Travers Block
(1870–1871)

Architect: Richard Morris Hunt

Architect Richard Morris Hunt designed the Stick Style commercial building for New Yorker William Travers. Hunt, the first American educated at the École des Beaux Arts (School of Fine Arts) in Paris, modeled the Travers Block after French medieval structures and the most innovative buildings in fashionable French seaside resorts, such as Deauville. Newport was transformed by Hunt, known as the "dean of American architecture." His numerous Newport cottages included Marble House (1892) and The Breakers (1895) for the Vanderbilt family.

Newport Casino *(photo c. 1890)*

4
Newport Casino (1879–1881)

Architects: McKim, Mead & White

The Casino is an early example of the Shingle Style perfected by the firm of McKim, Mead & White, which became one of the most acclaimed and successful design firms in American history. The commission established the national reputation of the architects and was among their earliest works. Newport's summer life immediately focused on the Casino's club rooms, tennis courts, theater, and stores. Today the building is home to the International Tennis Hall of Fame.

"The building is…dignified enough without being formal or pretentious; rural, but not rustic; graceful, intimate, cheerful, with just a touch of fantasy not out of place in a structure whose ends are distinctly frivolous…a Casino which is a mere summer house for 'society's' amusements."

Marianna Griswold van Rensselaer, "America's Country Dwellings," *The Century Magazine,* May 1886

24 BELLEVUE AVENUE • NEWPORT

King Block *(photo 2004)*

5
King Block
(1892–1893)

Architects: Perkins and Betton

The King family of Newport, owners of Kingscote and other houses on Bellevue Avenue, developed this block of stores. The Kings reinvested their China Trade fortune in Newport real estate, both in land and in commercial development, as the city grew into a premier summer resort in the late nineteenth century.

> "Newport's history belongs to all of you. All of you share the responsibility for your city's future.... Together you can make Newport one of the most interesting tourist centers in the United States. Together you can help preserve America's history in bricks and mortar and do a tremendously important service for the generations which will come after you.... Some of you may be saying, 'But do we want all these people swarming over Newport?' That is for you to decide—but may I remind you that a lot of things in Newport belong to these people. They are Americans, too, and Newport is part of their heritage"
>
> William Chorley, President of Colonial Williamsburg; excerpt from speech "Only Tomorrow" delivered to an assembly of Newport citizens convened under the auspices of The Preservation Society of Newport County, March 25, 1947

Audrain Building *(photo c. 1910)*

6
Audrain Building
(1902–1903)

Architect: Bruce Price

Glazed terra cotta in the style of the Italian Renaissance artist Andrea della Robbia decorates the facade of the Audrain Building. Copies of his swaddling infants from the Foundling Hospital in Florence, Italy, appear on the building, which served as medical offices. The architect, Bruce Price, also built several cottages in the fashionable community of Tuxedo Park, New York.

Detail, Audrain Building *(photo 2008)*

28 BELLEVUE AVENUE • NEWPORT

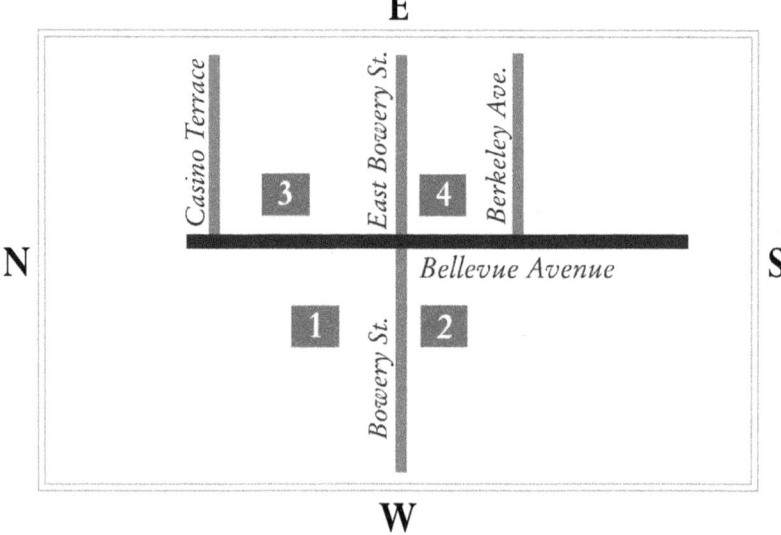

1. Kingscote
2. Elmcourt
3. Bellevue Plaza
4. Bellevue House

Kingscote
& Its Neighbors

Kingscote (1841) was the earliest summer cottage in Newport and began the "cottage boom," which continued until the early 1900s. Newport became the place to build the most innovative designs in American domestic architecture as the rich, fashionable, and famous hired the nation's leading designers to create summer villas. The cottage "boom" had gone "bust" by the 1950s, when modern development encroached on the neighborhood with the creation of shopping centers on the sites of historic buildings.

"Cottages–everything here is called a cottage–every variety of architecture. Swiss, Gothic, French, Elizabethan, and American, and of every degree of cost, from the humbler structure that is rented for a thousand a year up to the stately mansion in which hundreds of thousands are invested, line the spacious avenues."

"Newport," *Picturesque America*, edited by William Cullen Bryant, 1872

Kingscote *(photo c. 1875)*

1
Kingscote
(1839–1841)

Architect: Richard Upjohn
Addition by McKim, Mead & White (1881)

George Noble Jones, a prominent Georgia plantation owner, built this Gothic Revival style villa, which spurred the boom in summer cottage construction on a dirt road that became, in the early 1850s, fashionable Bellevue Avenue. Architect Richard Upjohn won the commission to remodel Trinity Church on Wall Street in New York after designing the Jones villa. In 1857, Upjohn became the first president of the newly founded American Institute of Architects. William Henry King, a wealthy China Trade merchant and member of a prominent Newport family, purchased the Jones villa in 1863. Four generations of the King family lived in the house. They renamed it Kingscote and added the dining room, one of the finest interiors in nineteenth-century America, designed by architects McKim, Mead & White with glass bricks by Louis Comfort Tiffany. The King family bequeathed Kingscote to The Preservation Society of Newport County in 1972.

Elmcourt *(photo c. 1874)*

2
Elmcourt
(1852–1853)

Architect / Builder: Original architect unknown
Remodeled by McKim, Mead & White (1882)
and Ogden Codman Jr. (1897)

Industrialist Andrew Robeson Jr. of Fall River, Massachusetts, built this Italianate villa. An abolitionist, Mr. Robeson was a conductor for the Underground Railroad, assisting slaves to freedom. The house has had several owners, including Francis Work of New York, a stockbrocker and business associate of Commodore Cornelius Vanderbilt, the founder of the New York Central Railroad. Through Work's daughter's marriage to Lord Fermoy, one of his descendants was Diana, Princess of Wales. The house remains a private residence.

34 BELLEVUE AVENUE • NEWPORT

First Ocean House Hotel *(print c. 1844)*

ABOVE: **Second Ocean House Hotel** *(print c. 1860)*

LEFT: **Second Ocean House fire** *(photo 1895)*

3
Bellevue Plaza
(1958)

Site of the first Ocean House Hotel (1841)
and second Ocean House Hotel (1845)

Architect: Russell Warren

The first and second Ocean House Hotels popularized Newport as a summer resort. As Newport evolved into a more socially exclusive resort by the 1850s, private cottages replaced hotels as the summer dwelling of choice. The first Greek Revivial style Ocean House Hotel burned in 1845. The Gothic Revival style selected for its replacement a year later reflected rapidly changing architectural tastes. After the second Ocean House Hotel burned in 1895, the lot remained empty until the creation of the Bellevue Avenue Shopping Plaza in 1958.

Bellevue Plaza
(photo 2009)

RIGHT: **Bellevue House**
(photo c. 1950)

LEFT: **Bellevue House and grounds**
(photo Kevin Rinaldi-Young, 2009)

BELOW: **Bellevue House**
(photo c. 1950)

Bellevue House (1909–1910)

Architect: Ogden Codman Jr.

Ogden Codman Jr. designed Berkeley Villa, a Colonial Revival style summer house, for his cousin, Martha Codman. He planned the gardens, which were later embellished by the noted French landscape architect Achille Duchêne. Codman had made his reputation with the design of the Vanderbilt family bedrooms of The Breakers (1895) and with the publication of *The Decoration of Houses* (1897) with his friend, the writer and Newport summer resident Edith Wharton. The book heralded the rejection of Victorian ornament in favor of classical forms. Martha Codman married the Russian tenor Maxim Karolik, three decades her junior. During their twenty-year marriage, they assembled important collections of eighteenth-century American furniture and nineteenth-century paintings and drawings, which they donated to the Museum of Fine Arts, Boston. Broadway star Jane Pickens purchased the estate in 1963, renaming it Bellevue House. Today it remains a private residence with continued additions of classical follies and landscape features. "Today, [the current owner], a noted preservationist and urban planner,... is currently involved in the renovation of the house and grounds, while preserving the beauty and integrity of the original Codman design.... He has created two new garden pavilions, both adapted from Samuel McIntire designs in Salem, Massachusetts.... These structures seamlessly integrate with the established architectural framework of the estate."

Michael Kathrens, *Newport Villas,* 2008

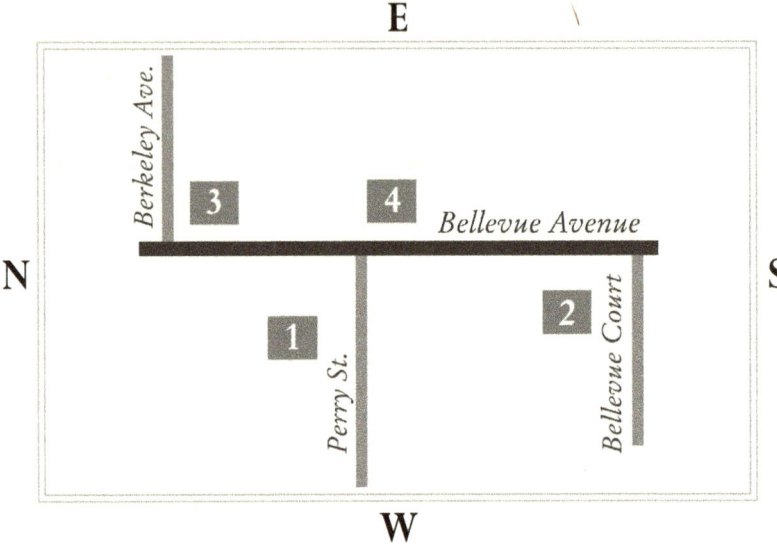

1. Isaac Bell House
2. East Court
3. LeRoy King House
4. C.H. Baldwin House

The Isaac Bell House
& Its Neighbors

During the 1870s and 1880s, architects pioneered a new type of American house based on a more open design and the use of organic materials. Queen Anne, Stick, and Shingle Style houses, with their half-timbering or rustic shingles, contrasted sharply with the ornate decoration and brilliant colors of earlier Victorian houses of the 1860s. The Isaac Bell House was a revolutionary design when it first appeared in 1883. The informality of its plan and use of natural wood shingles became the basic features of houses in the Shingle Style, which laid the foundation for modern American houses of the early 1900s by such notable architects as Frank Lloyd Wright.

> "One phase in American domestic architecture… the wooden, suburban building of the period 1872 to about 1889…developed…into a unique American achievement in architecture, one which has since been acclaimed by the whole world."
>
> Vincent J. Scully Jr., *The Stick and Shingle Style,* 1955

Isaac Bell House exterior and detail of dolphin porch bracket *(photo 2009)*

Interior detail. Breton woodwork, Isaac Bell House *(photo 2005)*

Detail. Japanese-inspired wallpaper, Isaac Bell House *(photo 2005)*

1
Isaac Bell House (1881–1883)

Architects: McKim, Mead & White

Isaac Bell, descended from a prominent colonial Connecticut family, retired at age thirty from the cotton brokerage business in New York City with a fortune he made, inherited, and acquired by marriage. His brother-in-law, James Gordon Bennett, was heir to the *New York Herald* newspaper empire and built the Newport Casino. Isaac Bell commissioned the new firm of McKim, Mead & White to build his Newport summer house just as the architects were completing the Casino. The building's open plan—partly inspired by traditional Japanese houses—and its organic relationship with the landscape made a revolutionary architectural statement in 1883. The patronage of Newport families like the Bells, Bennetts, and Kings fostered the innovative designs of McKim, Mead & White, who became one of the most fashionable and prolific architectural firms of the late nineteenth century. After a series of owners and a period as a nursing home, The Preservation Society of Newport County acquired the Isaac Bell House in 1994. It is now a National Historic Landmark.

East Court *(photo c. 2005)*

2
East Court
(c. 1855)

Architect / Builder: Original unknown
Remodeled by J.D. Johnston (1886–1887)

Coal magnate Edward Julius Berwind purchased the Italianate style East Court in 1912 as one of three adjacent guesthouses for his estate, The Elms (1901). Upon the dissolution of the Berwind estate, East Court was divided into two townhouses. Today the house is a single private residence.

> "But to the student of domestic architecture, Newport is the most interesting of our summer colonies.... Colonial houses are abundant.... Its newer portions show a characteristic instance of that way of [American] village planning...wide streets of detached houses, each with its own small lawn and garden, and all overshadowed by thickset and lofty trees."
>
> Marianna Griswold van Rensselaer, "American Country Dwellings," *The Century Magazine,* May 1886

44 Bellevue Avenue • NEWPORT

LeRoy King House *(photo 2009)*

3
LeRoy King House
(1884–1886)

Architects: McKim, Mead & White

LeRoy King, a member of the King family of Newport, selected McKim, Mead & White to build his villa in the Queen Anne Revival style. The architects had just completed the dining room of Kingscote one block north for his cousin, David King Jr., and a house for Isaac Bell across the street. With fortunes made in the China Trade, real estate, and finance, members of the King family began building impressive houses in this neighborhood in the 1840s and served as patrons of the finest American architects. LeRoy King's son, Frederick Rhinelander King, studied architecture at the École des Beaux Arts in Paris and worked for McKim, Mead & White before opening his own practice. The house is still a private residence.

> "Because the single-family house is an icon of our culture, we know the names of architects who have designed famous houses....But the art of architecture is realized in a physical and tangible dimension, and as works of art the houses of McKim, Mead & White constitute a portfolio of some of the most original and well-crafted designs produced in America."
>
> Samuel G. White, *The Houses of McKim, Mead & White*, 1998

C.H. Baldwin House *(photo 1950)*

4
C.H. Baldwin House (1877–1878)

Architects: Potter and Robertson

Rear Admiral Charles H. Baldwin built this Queen Anne revival style cottage and named it Snug Harbor. The sweeping gables, half-timbering, and open floor plans of Queen Anne Revival style houses of the 1870s laid the groundwork for the revolutionary designs of the Shingle Style of the 1880s. Admiral Baldwin's house was targeted in a well-publicized theft:

> *Another daring robbery, causing heavy loss, was successfully accomplished this evening in the cottage of Rear-Admiral Charles H. Baldwin.... About 7:15, while the Admiral and Mrs. Baldwin were entertaining a party of friends for dinner, noise was heard in the second story, and as no one should have been there servants went up stairs to see what was the matter. A glance showed that a robbery had been committed.... The cracksmen were experienced hands, having got through the roof into the second story. The loss is estimated at several thousand dollars.*
> —The New York Times, September 13, 1885

The robber, noted Chicago thief Charles Engle, was apprehended ten months later. The house remains a private residence.

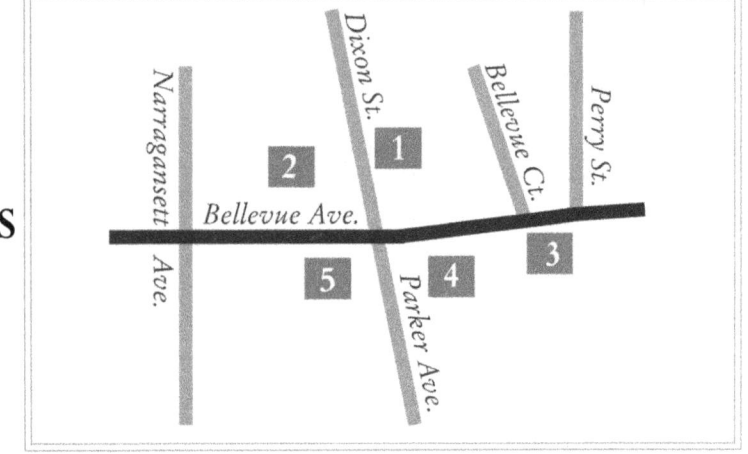

1. **The Elms**
2. **Villa Rosa** *(demolished)*
3. **deRham Cottage**
4. **William G. Weld House**
5. **Arleigh** *(demolished)*

"An auctioneer's ivory gavel sounded on this breezy blue afternoon in The Elms....The sale to settle the estate had legal, financial and social overtones that were pure Newport....The changes in Newport have also involved striking contrasts....The Elms looked today like a living museum. Villa Rosa, the adjacent home, looked exactly like a haunted house... Stoneacre, a few blocks away, is under demolition"

"Auction at Newport Tarnishes Some of the Grandeur That Was Newport," *The New York Times,* June 28, 1962

The Elms
& Its Neighbors

Demolition threatened The Elms and the surrounding summer houses in the 1960s, a critical period when the architectural landmarks of Bellevue Avenue were on the verge of complete destruction. In 1962, The Preservation Society of Newport County saved The Elms, while a developer demolished the neighboring Villa Rosa. Construction of new buildings not in sympathy with the historic setting was also an issue of concern. In 1965, the City of Newport created the Historic District in response to these events.

Aerial view of The Elms and its neighbors *(photo c. 1940)*

50 BELLEVUE AVENUE • NEWPORT

ABOVE: **The Elms**
(photo c. 1910)

LEFT: **Sunken Garden, The Elms**
(postcard c. 1920)

RIGHT: **Original cottage at The Elms**
(photo c. 1880)

7
The Elms
(1899–1901)

Architect: Horace Trumbauer

Pennsylvania coal magnate Edward Julius Berwind built this Classical Revival style French chateau, one of the grandest of Newport's Gilded Age houses and gardens. In 1899 Mr. Berwind demolished the original wooden cottage called The Elms to make way for his new house. The relatively simple wooden cottages of the mid-nineteenthth century that lined Bellevue Avenue were frequently remodeled or torn down due to a taste for more opulent houses in the 1890s. A developer purchased The Elms in 1961 with plans for commercial development. In 1962, The Preservation Society of Newport County saved The Elms from probable destruction. Today, The Elms is a National Historic Landmark.

ABOVE: **Ballroom, Villa Rosa**
(photo c. 1910)

RIGHT: **Entrance gates, Villa Rosa**
(photo c. 1910)

BELOW: **Villa Rosa**
(postcard c. 1910)

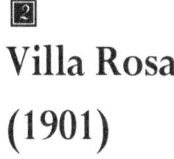
Villa Rosa
(1901)

Architect: Ogden Codman Jr.

Ogden Codman Jr., a friend of the writer and Newport summer resident Edith Wharton, designed this villa for E. Rollins Morse, a Boston banker and broker. E. Rollins Morse and Brothers were the Boston representatives of J.P. Morgan and Co., the most powerful bank of the Gilded Age. The estate occupied an entire block on Bellevue Avenue. A developer demolished Villa Rosa in 1962, prompting a major preservation outcry in Newport. A three-story apartment complex was built on the site in 1965. In 2004, the condominium association approved the demolition of the gates, one of the last surviving original features of the 1901 estate, generating public criticism.

> **"If proportion is the good breeding of architecture, symmetry may be defined as the sanity of decoration."**
>
> Ogden Codman Jr. and Edith Wharton, *The Decoration of Houses,* 1897

deRham Cottage *(photo 2004)*

3
deRham Cottage
(c. 1860)

Architect: Unknown

Henry Casimir deRham was a successful banker and merchant in New York who founded the Swiss Benevolent Society of New York in 1832. The second Empire style deRham cottage was moved to its present site in 1882 to make way for William G. Weld's new estate directly to the south. The square wooden cottage with a Mansard roof was one of the most popular building types in Newport during the 1860s. Many of these cottages were demolished in the late nineteenth and early twentieth centuries to make way for palatial mansions.

> "Newport was for the eating of dinners and the batting of balls, for dancing, yachting and for strutting; Newport was for July and August and the exchange of visits that were in themselves both ends and means."
>
> Louis Auchincloss, introduction to *Newport Pleasures and Palaces* by Nancy Sirkis, 1963

William G. Weld House *(photo c. 1890)*

4
William G. Weld House
(1882–1884)

Architect: Dudley Newton

Newport architect Dudley Newton designed this Queen Anne Revival style villa for prominent Bostonian William G. Weld. The Weld family fortune was based on merchant shipping and railroad stocks. Members of the Weld family were important collectors of Japanese art and major donors to the Museum of Fine Arts, Boston. William Weld was on the first board of the Massachusetts Society for the Prevention of Cruelty to Animals with John Quincy Adams and Ralph Waldo Emerson. In 1924 the house became De la Salle Academy, a Roman Catholic school for boys. In 1973 it was converted to condominiums, with new units added to the historic grounds.

"Mr. Weld was in no sense a club man and he entertained only in the circle of his more immediate friends. While a thorough Bostonian, his name is hardly less well known in this city. He owned a magnificent stone residence on Bellevue Avenue, where it was his custom to spend about seven months of the year. One of his most notable public benefactions was the erection of the statue on Touro Park in memory of Dr. William Ellery Channing."

Newport Mercury, April 18, 1896

58 Bellevue Avenue • NEWPORT

Arleigh *(photo c. 1900)*

Arleigh
(1891–1893)

Architect: J.D. Johnston

This Queen Anne Revival style villa was home to many prominent Newport summer residents. Arleigh was the setting for the 1903 wedding of Cathleen Gebhard Neilson to Reginald Claypoole Vanderbilt, whose family established the New York Central Railroad and built The Breakers as their Newport summer house. In the early 20th century, Harry Symes Lehr and his wife Elizabeth Drexel Lehr, resided at Arleigh. Mrs. Lehr's memoir, *King Lehr and the Gilded Age* (1935), provides a window onto Gilded Age society. Arleigh was destroyed by fire in 1932. The lot was vacant until construction of the Heatherwood Nursing Facility in 1972. Many of the estate's fine specimen trees from the 1890s survive today.

"The palaces of Newport are architectural backgrounds for the pleasures and sports of its inhabitants."

Barr Ferree, on Newport, *American Estates and Gardens*, 1904

1. 424 Bellevue Avenue
2. Chateau Nooga
3. Rockry Hall
4. Maplehurst
5. Lindenhurst
6. The Villa
7. Wayside
8. White Lodge

424 Bellevue
& Its Neighbors

The corner of Bellevue and Narragansett Avenues served as the assembly point for the Coaching Club annual meeting, a great social occasion for Newport's summer residents begun in 1888. Fine horses, carriages, and perfectly groomed passengers made up one of the grandest events on Bellevue Avenue. By the 1940s, the grandeur of Newport's Gilded Age past was gone and the avenue was severely deteriorated. Due to increased taxes and changing lifestyles, many private owners sold their houses or donated them to charitable or educational institutions. The time had come to adapt to the future. With the restoration of its historic roadbed in 1992 and a mixed use of private residences and non-profit institutions, Bellevue Avenue has regained its historical residential character and looks much as it did when the street hosted the afternoon drives of the famous and the fashionable in the late nineteenth century.

> **"Bellevue Avenue, the address of the famous mansions, has been restored...at a cost of 7 million. Cracked pavement has been replaced with a smooth road that duplicated the 1890s original."**
>
> "Newport Salutes Restored Avenue," *The New York Times,* May 31, 1992

424 Bellevue *(photo 2004)*

1
424 Bellevue Avenue (1887)

Architects: Harding and Dinkelberg

William Osgood, with a fortune in North Carolina zinc, built this Romanesque Revival style villa. The Honorary Herbert C. Pell and his family lived in the house during the 1920s and 1930s. Herbert Pell's son, Claiborne, served as a U.S. Senator from Rhode Island from 1961 to 1997. The Pell family donated the house to the Roman Catholic Diocese of Providence for use as St. Catherine's Academy (1941–1971). Later the City of Newport used the house as an elementary school and leased it as classroom space to Salve Regina University. In 1992 The Preservation Society of Newport County acquired the building for its headquarters, thus securing the historic character of a highly visible intersection on Bellevue Avenue.

> "I have grown up seeing the wonderful things accomplished by this organization. So I am sure it is your work in great part that made me become so interested in the restoration and preservation of our national shrines."
>
> Jacqueline Kennedy, telegram sent to Mrs. George Henry Warren, President of The Preservation Society of Newport County, upon Mrs. Kennedy's receipt of The Preservation Society's Award for Outstanding Contribution in the Field of the Decorative Arts, 1962

Chateau Nooga *(photo c. 1950)*

Chateau Nooga
(1880–1881)

Architect: George Brown Post

Christopher Columbus Baldwin, president of the Nashville Railroad, built this Queen Anne Revival style house. The architect, George Brown Post, later designed the New York Stock Exchange. Chateau Nooga was featured in *L'Architecture Americaine* (1886) by André Daly fils et. Cie. It was one of two buildings from Rhode Island included in the volume, which highlighted contemporary American architecture.

> "The afternoon drive, usually down Bellevue to Ocean Avenue...is a superb pageant of carriages, handsome women, elegant men and graceful children."
>
> "The Queen of Aquidneck,"
> *Harper's New Monthly Magazine,* August 1874

Rockry Hall *(photo c. 1910)*

3
Rockry Hall
(1847–1848)

Architect: Seth Bradford

Built for Albert Sumner of Boston, Rockry Hall is one of the early Gothic Revival style houses on Bellevue Avenue. Albert Sumner's brother, Charles, was a U.S. Senator from Massachusetts from 1851 to 1874. Senator Sumner was a prominent abolitionist and, in one of the more shocking events of pre–Civil War Washington, was severely beaten on the Senate floor by South Carolina Representative Preston Brooks after an anti slavery speech. Seth Bradford was a noted builder of some of Newport's early summer houses, such as Chateau-sur-Mer (1852) and Fairlawn (1853) on Bellevue Avenue. Rockry Hall and the neighboring Shingle style house known as Dellmain, by architect Daniel Curry, were joined after 1889.

68 Bellevue Avenue • NEWPORT

Maplehurst *(photo 2004)*

4
Maplehurst (William Starr Miller House) (1881–1883)

Architects: Attributed to McKim, Mead & White

New York banker William Starr Miller commissioned Maplehurst. This house is one of a group of innovative Shingle Style designs that Newport architects perfected during the early 1880s. Shingle Style houses were inspired by historic features from Colonial America, Britain, Europe, and the Far East, but used details and materials in innovative ways. Originally the style was referred to as the "modernized colonial" by George Sheldon in *Artistic Country Seats* (1886), because of its original approach to using historic features. The architectural historian Vincent Scully coined the term "Shingle Style" in the 1940s.

> The ladies and gentlemen are in great force –the ladies, of course, especially. It is true everywhere, I suppose, that women are the animating element of "society;" but you feel this to be especially true as you pass along Bellevue Avenue."
>
> Henry James, *Portraits of Places,* 1883

Lindenhurst *(photo 2004)*

5
Lindenhurst
(1887–1888)

Architect: Unknown

John M. Hodgson, the premier florist in Gilded Age Newport, lived at Lindenhurst. The house is in the French Renaissance Revival style. Extensive greenhouses and cutting gardens once surrounded the estate. Mr. Hodgson was responsible for creating extravagant displays for houses such as The Elms (1901) and Rosecliff (1902).

> "All along Bellevue Avenue...are geraniums, roses, begonias, heliotropes, hydrangeas, verbenas, gladioli, a wilderness of flowers, native and exotic, filling the air with perfume and the eye with beauty."
>
> "The Queen of Aquidneck,"
> *Harper's New Monthly Magazine,* August 1874

The Villa *(photo 2004)*

6
The Villa
(1863–1864)

Architect: George Champlin Mason Sr.

Mary Sigourney of Boston built this Second Empire style villa. The architect, George Champlin Mason, was a historian and painter who helped develop Newport as a fashionable summer resort in the 1860s. Mason served as publisher and editor of the *Newport Mercury*. In 1875, he published *Newport and Its Cottages*, which documented more than 40 Newport houses.

> **"The villas and 'cottages,' the beautiful idle women, the beautiful idle men, the brilliant pleasure—fraught days and evenings, impart, perhaps, to Newport life a faintly European expression."**
>
> Henry James, *Portraits of Places,* 1883

Wayside *(photo 2004)*

Wayside
(1863)

Architect: George Champlin Mason Sr.
Remodeled by J.D. Johnston (1903)

Wayside was the summer residence of Elisha Dyer Jr., who served as Governor of Rhode Island from 1897 to 1900. Elisha Dyer, along with his neighbor Lispenard Stewart, was noted as one of the best-dressed gentlemen in Gilded Age Newport and as one of the city's most accomplished dancers. In 1903, architect J.D. Johnston remodeled this Second Empire style house in the Georgian Revival style.

"The principal social event to-night was the dinner dance given by Mr. and Mrs. E.J. Berwind at The Elms.... The cotillion was led by Elisha Dyer, Jr. with Mrs. Berwind."

"The News of Newport," *The New York Times,* September 11, 1904

White Lodge *(photo 2006)*

⑧
White Lodge
(1863–1864)

Architect: George Champlin Mason Sr.

This Second Empire style house was remodeled around 1900 with a Classical Revival style front porch. The ballroom was decorated by the English artist Walter Crane. Lispenard Stewart, a bachelor, was the most notable resident of White Lodge. A leading member of old New York's financial and social elite, Stewart was listed as 108 in Mrs. Astor's famous list of "the 400" in ultrafashionable society. One of the great dancers of the Gilded Age, Stewart led Miss Gertrude Vanderbilt in her first dance at her Newport debut in the summer of 1895 at The Breakers.

> "Behind the line of villas runs the Avenue, with more villas yet – of which there is nothing at all to say but that those built recently are a hundred times prettier than those built fifteen years ago, and give one some hope of a revival of the architectural art."
>
> Henry James, *Portraits of Places,* 1883

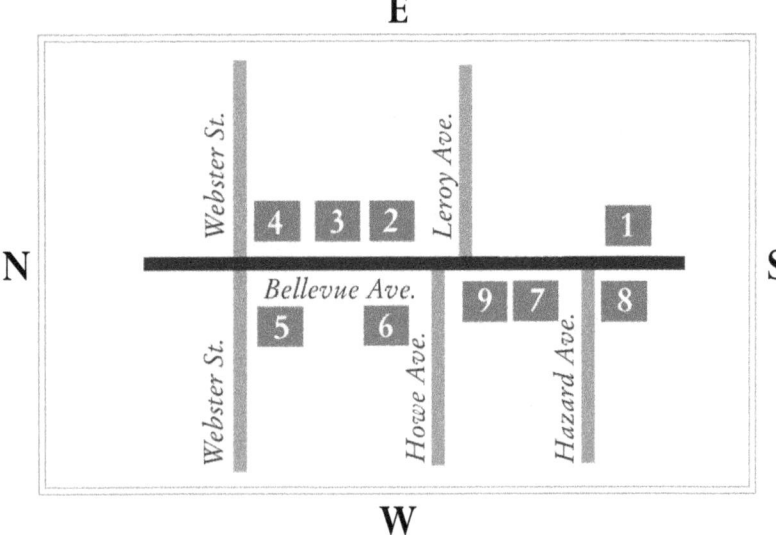

1. Chateau-sur-Mer
2. Flower Cottage
3. Wisteria Lodge
4. 446 Bellevue Avenue
5. Swanhurst
6. Knight Cottage
7. Harold Brown Villa
8. John Carter Brown House
9. Timmy "The Woodhooker's" Cottage *(demolished)*

Chateau-sur-Mer
& Its Neighbors

The buildings surrounding Chateau-sur-Mer capture the spirit of Newport in the High Victorian era. This block preserves one of the greatest concentrations of Victorian architecture and landscape design in Newport from the period 1850 to 1890. The residents of these houses, many related through marriage, were powerful merchants and bankers who later entered public service as senators, governors, mayors, and judges. The grounds of Chateau-sur-Mer and the Harold Brown Villa across the street were laid out by the Olmsted firm, founded by Frederick Law Olmsted, the designer of New York's Central Park. The natural style of Olmsted's landscapes is complemented by trees imported from Asia, Europe, and all parts of the Americas, reflecting the great Victorians' desire to collect the finest specimens from around the world. This architectural and landscape heritage was threatened in the 1960s as houses were auctioned for possible development. At the center of this architectural and landscape splendor was Mr. Sullivan's legendary junkyard, causing heated debate among Newporters about maintaining Bellevue Avenue's pristine character or respecting the rights of individuals to do as they wished on their own land.

Chateau-sur-Mer *(photo c. 1880)*

7

Chateau-sur-Mer (1851–1852)

Architect: Seth Bradford (1851)
Remodeling by Richard Morris Hunt (1871–1880)
and John Russell Pope (1914)

Chateau-sur-Mer was built for the Wetmore family, who were successful China Trade merchants. George Peabody Wetmore served as Governor of Rhode Island (1885–1887) and as a United States Senator (1895–1913). In 1966, Miss Edith Wetmore left Chateau-sur-Mer to the Society for the Preservation of New England Antiquities, which declined the bequest. This led to the auction of the estate and its collections. The Preservation Society saved Chateau-sur-Mer and its 17 acres with rare trees when threatened by development in 1969. Today the house is a National Historic Landmark.

> "Our task now is to communicate what we felt in seeing the need to save the Hunter House from demolition; to save The Elms from becoming a shopping center; to save Chateau-sur-Mer and its lovely grounds from being developed into a bevy of house lots....Our vision is one that sees the City-by-the-Sea, once famed for its material opulence, as a center for the arts, for architecture, for music and for literature."
>
> Mrs. George Henry Warren, *President's Report,* The Preservation Society of Newport County, 1970

Flower Cottage *(photo c. 1900)*

2
Flower Cottage
(c. 1882)

Architect: Clarence Sumner Luce

The Shingle Style Flower Cottage served as the store for the famed florist John M. Hodgson, who lived at Lindenhurst. The flower shop was converted to a private house in the Colonial Revival style in 1921.

> "The history of Newport architecture from the eighteen-forties to the twentieth century can be told only in terms of summer cottages and resort building."

Antoinette Downing and Vincent Scully, *The Architectural Heritage of Newport, Rhode Island,* 1952

84 BELLEVUE AVENUE • NEWPORT

Wisteria Lodge *(photo 2006)*

3
Wisteria Lodge
(1865)

Architect: Unknown

Wisteria Lodge was the residence of Jebez C. Knight, who served as Mayor of Providence, Rhode Island from 1859 to 1864. Other residents included Oliver C. Harriman of the powerful New York banking family, founders of the Harriman National Bank and Brown Brothers Harriman private bank. It was also the summer residence of philanthropist Evelyn Annenberg Hall.

> "Yet the houses of Newport are most important to the gay doings of this beautiful city; for the life of Newport is concerned solely with pleasure and with entertainment, and fine houses, richly furnished and decorated, spacious and elegant, built and adorned with a delightful disregard of cost and expense, with beautiful grounds arranged in a sumptuous fashion – these are the requirements, and the legitimate requirements of Newport palaces."
>
> Barr Ferree, on Newport, *American Estates and Gardens*, 1904

446 Bellevue (photo 2004)

4
446 Bellevue Avenue (c. 1850)

Architect: Unknown

The original Greek Revival style house on this site dates to the early 1800s. It was part of an extensive farm subdivided in the mid-nineteenth century to accommodate the boom in summer cottage construction. Subsequent owners remodeled the house during the course of the nineteenth and twentieth centuries.

> "They stand in stately rows along Bellevue Avenue in Newport, RI, once 'the richest street in the world.' Since the passing of the Gilded Age that these houses symbolized, two wars, a long depression, high income taxes and a shortage of servants have dimmed Newport's splendor. The doors of these villas will never be opened again."
>
> "Life Visits a Fading Newport," *Life* magazine, October 16, 1944

Swanhurst *(photo c. 1910)*

5
Swanhurst
(1851)

Architect: Alexander MacGregor

Alexander MacGregor built this Italianate style villa for Judge Gustavus Swann. Born on a farm in New Hampshire, Gustavus Swann studied law and moved to Ohio, where he became a successful lawyer and president of several banks. Judge Swann's daughter, Sara Rives, bequeathed Swanhurst to the Newport Art Association in 1928, which created the Swanhurst Art School in 1932 as a gathering place for Newport artists. The Players Guild, Rhode Island Shakespeare Theater, and Swanhurst Chorus performed in the theater in the estate carriage house. Swanhurst was sold in 1987 for conversion into a private residence.

> "The line of sumptuous villas –'The cottages', as they were ironically called by their inhabitants – which stretched the length of Bellevue Avenue along the cliffs and over Ochre Point, was Newport's glory."
>
> Lady Decies, *King Lehr and The Gilded Age*, 1935

Knight Cottage *(photo 2004)*

6
Knight Cottage (Mary Bruen House) (1882–1883)

Architect: William Ralph Emerson

Knight Cottage was built for the widow and children of the Reverend Matthias Bruen of New York. The Bruens' daughter Frances married Charles Callahan Perkins, a noted painter and illustrator, a founder and director of the Museum of Fine Arts, Boston, and president of the Boston Art Club. The architect of this Shingle Style house was the cousin of the writer Ralph Waldo Emerson.

> "But Newport represented the escape from duty into an atmosphere of unmitigated holiday-making."
>
> Edith Wharton, *The Age of Innocence*, 1920

Harold Brown Villa *(photo 2006)*

7
Harold Brown Villa (1893–1894)

Architect: Dudley Newton

Heir to one of the great Rhode Island fortunes, Harold Brown built his house on the lot next to his parents' house. His wife's uncle, George Peabody Wetmore, lived across the street at Chateau-sur-Mer. The Browns assembled an important collection of Napoleonic furniture and memorabilia for their Newport house and hired Ogden Codman Jr. to design a series of Empire style interiors. Mrs. Brown bequeathed her collection of Napoleonic objects to the Museum of the Rhode Island School of Design.

> "A community of wealth and pleasure, Newport is the chief city in the United States in which these characteristics are thoroughly dominant. The social aspects of this summer capital – for its in-gatherings of pleasure-loving people are truly national – are known of all men; but the highly important fact that this great social activity needs and necessitates an architectural background, a habitat, a scene and setting commensurate with its splendid pleasures, is less generally recognized or certainly very much less heard of."
>
> Barr Ferree, on Newport, *American Estates and Gardens*, 1904

John Carter Brown House *(photo 2004)*

8
Cannon Hill (John Carter Brown House) (before 1866)

Architect: George Champlin Mason Sr.
Remodeled by Carpenter & Childs

The Browns were one of Rhode Island's preeminent families, with a lineage and fortune dating to the colonial era. This Italianate villa was the summer residence of John Carter Brown. The elaborate curved center gable, large brackets supporting the cornices, and the round arched windows of the cupola are typical features of the Italianate style. John Carter Brown, whose father was the namesake of Brown University in Providence, RI, became a great collector of books and manuscripts on the Americas. His collection became the basis for the renowned John Carter Brown Library at Brown University. The house is a private residence.

Timmy "The Woodhooker's" Cottage *(photo c. 1950)*

9
Timmy "The Woodhooker's" Cottage (c. 1912)

Architect: Unknown

Timmy and Julia Sullivan operated a junkyard on the grounds of their historic cottage, causing much controversy among those who wished to maintain Bellevue Avenue's manicured character. After the Sullivans' deaths, the property was acquired by the adjacent Harold Brown estate in 1971, and the house was subsequently demolished.

> "The battle over the famous, if untidy, Sullivan junkyard is shaping up again...anybody going anywhere in Newport is bound to pass the Sullivan premises. It nestles in shoddy disarray among marble palaces and manicured lawns.... Mrs. Peyton Jaudon Van Rensselaer marshaled the forces of wealth and tidiness in an effort to turn the trick. She cited...the piled up lumber on sacrosanct Bellevue Avenue's sidewalks and the mosquito breeding puddles.... Only 15 nearby property owners would sign her petition for legal action. Among the refusers was Mrs. Cornelius Vanderbilt.... The mayor and city solicitor backed the Sullivans too, as did Mrs. Harold Brown, owner of the next door estate, who said she'd 'never put anyone out of his home.' The case never reached court."
>
> "Face-Lifting for Newport," *The American Weekly*, on the battle over Timmy "The Woodhooker" Sullivan's junkyard on historic Bellevue Avenue, July 13, 1947

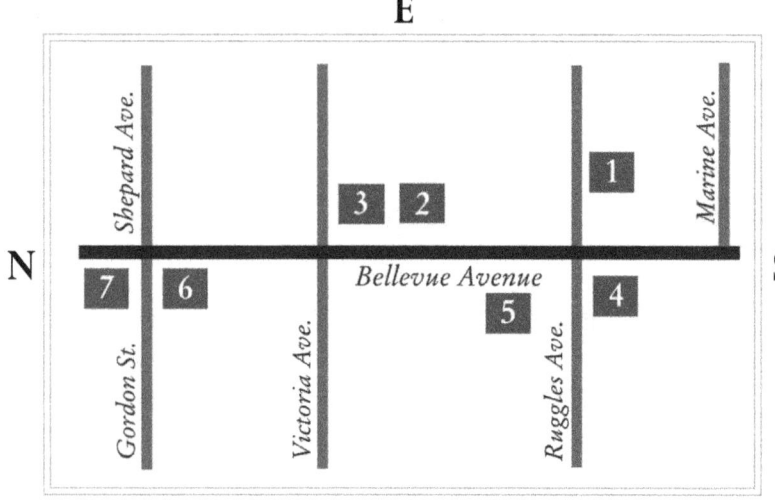

1. Fairlawn
2. Stoneacre *(demolished)*
3. Vernon Court
4. Belmead
5. Chetwode *(demolished)*
6. d'Hauteville Cottage
7. Stonor Lodge

Fairlawn
& Its Neighbors

The story of the houses on this block is one of shifting uses and continual remodeling by successive generations. Most of these houses were transformed from Victorian villas into grander mansions. During the 1960s and 1970s, the Stoneacre and Chetwode estates burned and were demolished, radically changing the appearance of this section of Bellevue Avenue. Today, the Fairlawn estate and more than twenty five other historic buildings have been incorporated into the campus of Salve Regina University, a coeducational institution for the liberal arts and sciences.

> "A small stroll through the campus of Salve Regina is a tour of the great architectural works of the Gilded Age. The protection and sensitive adaptation of these estates and their surrounding landscapes for educational use are examples of preservation at its best."
>
> Richard Moe, President, National Trust for Historic Preservation, 2006

100 Bellevue Avenue • NEWPORT

Fairlawn *(photo c. 1890)*

7
Fairlawn
(1852–1853)

Architect: Seth Bradford
Addition by Richard Morris Hunt (1869)
Remodeled by McKim, Mead & White (1880) and
Peabody and Stearns (1891)

Fairlawn is one of the most remodeled summer cottages in Newport. It began as an Elizabethan style cottage by contractor Seth Bradford. In the 1890s, Fairlawn became a Queen Anne Revival style villa after remodeling by such famous architects as Richard Morris Hunt and McKim, Mead & White. Levi P. Morton, a self-made dry goods merchant and banker and Vice President of the United States under President Benjamin Harrison, lived at Fairlawn during the late nineteenth century. Salve Regina University purchased the estate in 1997. The structure, now named the Young Building for University benefactors Anita O'keefe and Robert R. Young, houses the Pell Center for International Relations and Public Policy, named in honor of Rhode Island's esteemed Senator, Claiborne deBorda Pell.

102 BELLEVUE AVENUE • NEWPORT

Stoneacre *(photo c. 1888)*

2
Stoneacre
(1882–1885)

Architect: William Appleton Potter

John W. Ellis, an Ohio banker and manager of the Northern Pacific Railroad, built this Shingle Style house. Legendary landscape architect Frederick Law Olmsted, designer of New York's Central Park, planned the grounds. A fire in 1960 damaged the house and it was demolished in 1962. Vernon Court Junior College intended to build academic buildings on the site, but construction ceased after they declared bankruptcy in 1973. The grounds are now a private park dedicated in memory of Frederick Law Olmsted.

> **"The air and climate of Newport are secure assets."**
>
> Frederick Law Olmsted,
> Proposed Improvements for Newport, 1913

104 BELLEVUE AVENUE • NEWPORT

ABOVE: **Vernon Court** *(photo c. 1950)*

BELOW: **Matthews House** *(photo c. 1875)*

3

Vernon Court
(1898–1901)

Architects: Carrère and Hastings

The Classical Revival style Vernon Court replaced an earlier Stick Style house built in 1872 for Nathan Matthews. Carrère and Hastings started their career in the architectural office of McKim, Mead & White. After establishing their own firm, they became distinguished for their Classical Revival style buildings, including the New York Public Library. From 1956 until the early 1970s Vernon Court, along with several nearby properties including Stoneacre, served as a preparatory school. The house is now a private residence and home to the National Museum of American Illustration.

"The startling and daring originality…give it high rank among the notable houses of America. It is one of the most individual mansions in Newport: a house of refined beauty, admirably studied in all its parts, yet of truly spontaneous design."

Barr Ferree, on Vernon Court, *American Estates and Gardens*, 1904

Belmead *(photo 2009)*

4
Belmead
(1895)

Architect: Bruce Price

New York financier George S. Scott and his wife built the Georgian Revival style Belmead, originally in brick with stone trim. Subsequent owners stuccoed the building and painted it white. The U.S. government purchased Belmead for naval officers' housing during World War II. The building had several owners after the 1940s, among them Salve Regina University, which used it as a student dormitory. Belmead is now condominiums.

> "The common plywood tacked across the windows of the grand homes used by the now closed Vernon Court Junior College scars the splendor of the surrounding architecture of Newport's Golden Age."
>
> "Bellevue Avenue–Can Grandeur Be Saved?"
> *Providence Journal,* April 23, 1972

108 BELLEVUE AVENUE • NEWPORT

ABOVE: **Pansy Cottage** *(photo 1895)*
BELOW: **Chetwode garden facade** *(photo c. 1920)*

5
Chetwode
(1900–1903)

Architect: Horace Trumbauer

William Storrs Wells lived in Pansy Cottage, designed by architect Richard Morris Hunt, until the house was destroyed by fire in 1900. Philadelphia architect Horace Trumbauer, designer of The Elms (1901), replaced Pansy Cottage with Chetwode, a grand house inspired by seventeenth-and eighteenth-century French chateaux. In 1934, John Jacob Astor III purchased Chetwode. The house and its contents were put up for auction in 1948. The property passed through a series of owners until 1972. In January of that year a fire caused extensive damage. The house was demolished in 1973, and the lavish French-style gardens were subdivided into house lots in 1976.

> "Newport, at all events, illustrates splendid living in the most splendid fashion it has yet attained in America, so far as a group of houses and a group of people are concerned."
>
> Barr Ferree, on Newport, *American Estates and Gardens*, 1904

ABOVE: **d'Hauteville Cottage** *(photo c. 1875)*
BELOW: **Remains of d'Hauteville Cottage** *(photo 2009)*

d'Hauteville Cottage (c. 1871)

Architects: Peabody and Stearns

Harvard graduate and Civil War captain Frederick S.C. Hauteville was the son of a Swiss aristocrat and a Boston socialite. Hauteville was involved in a landmark custody case, notable because guardianship was awarded to his mother, Ellen Sears Grand d'Hauteville, at a time when judicial law favored paternal claims. In the early 1870s, Hauteville commissioned noted Boston architects Peabody and Stearns to design a Stick Style villa. During the 1900s, the house was dramatically downsized due to renovations by subsequent owners. The original sprawling villa is unrecognizable today.

"How sensible they ought to be, the denizens of these pleasant places, of their peculiar felicity and distinction! How it should purify their temper and refine their tastes! How delicate, how wise, how discriminating they should become! What excellent manners – what enlightened opinions – their situation should produce! How it should purge them of vulgarity! Happy villeggiannti of Newport."

Henry James, *Portraits of Places*, 1883

Stonor Lodge *(photo c. 1915)*

7
Stonor Lodge

Architect: Unknown
Remodeled by George Champlin Mason Sr. (1866) and
Dudley Newton (1880)

Stonor Lodge evolved from an eighteenth-century farmhouse (c. 1793) into a fashionable Newport summer cottage when the land was subdivided for development by Henry Tiffany in 1840. In 1866, Newport architect George Champlin Mason Sr. made alterations to the building. Dudley Newton remodeled the house in the Stick Style in 1880. The house remains a private residence.

> "The fact is, they want to try Newport this summer, and if I can make it a success for them they—well, they'll make it a success for me."
>
> Edith Wharton, *The House of Mirth*, 1905

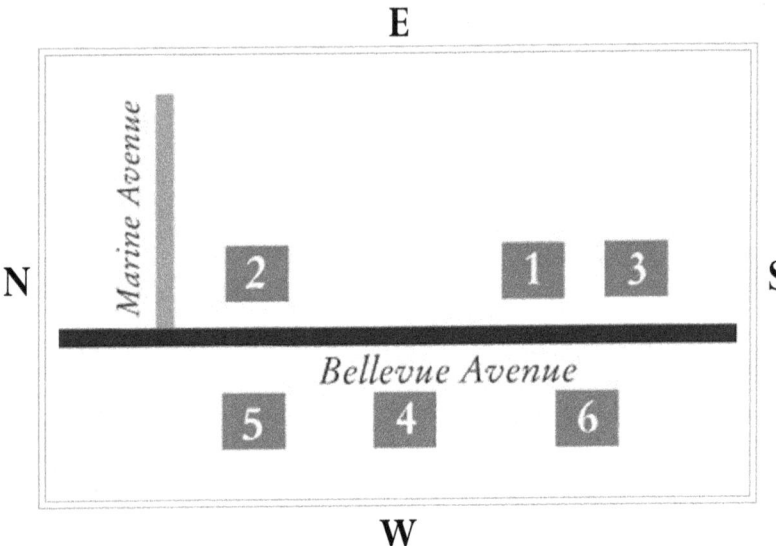

1. Rosecliff
2. By-the-Sea *(demolished)*
3. Seacliff
4. Sunnylea
5. Ivy Tower
6. Sherwood

Rosecliff
& Its Neighbors

The 1940s brought enormous change to houses on this block of Bellevue Avenue as Gilded Age glamour faded due to demolitions, fire, and acquisition of many properties for use by schools. Increasing income and real estate taxes and a changing lifestyle in post–World War II America made the grand houses of Newport appear as relics from another era. Newport was seen as a fading beauty. Built in 1902 for an estimated $2 million, Rosecliff sold in 1941 for only $21,000. Whitney Cottage, to the north of Rosecliff, burned in 1942. The Hatch Preparatory School and Vernon Court Junior College acquired many houses in the 1960s at a time when they were viewed as expensive tax burdens and no longer practical as private residences. By the 1980s, a revival of the block occurred due to a renewed interest in ownership of historic estates.

"Among all Newport's stately summer palaces, Rosecliff stood out as one of the most glittering white elephants of them all.... Theresa Fair Oelrichs began building Rosecliff when there were already some mighty mansions to surpass.... Into Rosecliff she packed what Henry James called the 'loot of Europe'.... Last week, house and furnishing were auctioned."

"The Dismantling of Newport," *TIME*, July 28, 1941

116 BELLEVUE AVENUE • NEWPORT

ABOVE: **Rosecliff** *(photo c. 1910)*
BELOW: **Bancroft House** *(photo c. 1880)*

Rosecliff
(1899–1902)

Architects: McKim, Mead & White

To make way for a grander Rosecliff, Theresa Fair Oelrichs purchased and demolished the wooden cottage (c. 1852) of George Bancroft, a noted diplomat, historian, and horticulturalist famed for his roses. A Nevada silver heiress, Mrs. Oelrichs hired noted architects McKim, Mead & White to create this rendition of the Grand Trianon (1697), King Louis XIV's retreat in the gardens of his palace at Versailles. Some of Gilded Age Newport's most spectacular parties took place at Rosecliff, such as the White Ball of 1906, when Mrs. Oelrichs moored a fleet of white mock ships off the coast. In 1913, Mrs. Oelrichs dressed as Mother Goose to greet guests to her Fairy Tales Ball. In 1941, the Oelrichs family sold Rosecliff to singer Gertrude Neissen for $21,000. Left unattended, the house suffered severe water damage. Mr. Ray Alan Van Clief carefully repaired Rosecliff but was killed in an automobile accident en route to spending his first night at the house. Mr. and Mrs. J. Edgar Monroe of New Orleans, the last private owners of Rosecliff, donated the house to the Preservation Society in 1971. Rosecliff's romantic and theatrical qualities made it a perfect setting for motion pictures, such as *The Great Gatsby* (1973).

118 BELLEVUE AVENUE • NEWPORT

TOP: **By-the-Sea**
(photo c. 1930)

RIGHT: **By-the-Sea**
(photo c. 1880)

BOTTOM: **Parterre**
(photo 2008)

2
By-the-Sea
(1860)

Architect: George Champlin Mason Sr.

Mr. and Mrs. August Belmont built this Italianate style villa. Mr. Belmont, originally from Germany, was a U.S. agent of the powerful Rothschild bank. His wife, Caroline, was a daughter of Newport's Commodore Matthew Perry, who opened the ports of Japan to American trade in 1854. The Belmonts were the first to bring glamour and grand living to Newport in the 1860s as the town became a fashionable summer resort. The worldly August Belmont and the celebrated beauty of his wife inspired the fictional couple the Beauforts in Edith Wharton's 1921 Pulitzer Prize–winning novel *The Age of Innocence,* which used Newport's cottages as a backdrop. The Belmonts' son August Jr. depleted his fortune by investing in the New York subway system and the Cape Cod Canal, later bought by the U.S. government. The Belmonts' second son, Oliver Hazard Perry Belmont, married Alva Vanderbilt after her 1895 divorce from W.K. Vanderbilt. By-the-Sea was demolished in 1946. Parterre (1999) now occupies this site.

The Reefs *(photo c. 1910)*

13
Seacliff
(1953)

Architect: Frederick Rhinelander King

Christopher Wolfe of New York built an Italianate house called The Reefs on this site in 1853. Mr. and Mrs. Harry Payne Whitney owned the house from 1896 to 1942. Mrs. Whitney was born Gertrude Vanderbilt, daughter of Cornelius Vanderbilt II, of The Breakers (1895). She became a noted sculptor and founded the Whitney Museum of American Art in New York. Her modernist studio (1939) still stands on Cliff Walk at the edge of this property. Newport architect Frederick Rhinelander King designed the present Colonial Revival style house called Seacliff in 1953 for Mr. and Mrs. Reginald B. Rives.

> "…we proceeded in state down Bellevue Avenue. And society rolled by in the elegant equipages one saw in those days when to be well turned out on wheels with a handsome pair of horses was as necessary to one's standard of luxury as a fine house."

Consuelo Vanderbilt Balsan, writing on life in Newport in the 1890s, *The Glitter and the Gold*, 1953

Sunnylea *(photo c. 1890)*

4
Sunnylea
(1881–1882)

Architect: Dudley Newton

Mr. and Mrs. Charles F. Chickering of New York built the Queen Anne Revival style Sunnylea. Mr. Chickering worked with his father, Jonas, the founder of the famed Chickering Piano Company. Newport architect Dudley Newton received his first grand house commission with the Sunnylea project. Newton apprenticed with George Champlin Mason, a builder of many Newport summer houses and author of *Newport and Its Cottages* (1875). Typical of many Newport houses, Sunnylea had several owners, including the Hatch Preparatory School (1959–1961) and Vernon Court Junior College (1964–1970). Today the house is a private residence.

> "America's discovery of her own past was bound to bring Newport again into the public eye, for it is a textbook, in bricks and mortar, of much of our history."
>
> Louis Auchincloss, introduction, *Newport Pleasures and Palaces* by Nancy Sirkis, 1963

Ivy Tower *(photo 2006)*

Ivy Tower
(1887–1888)

Architect: J.D. Johnston

Harriet Pond was one of eight New Yorkers building houses in 1887 during Newport's cottage construction boom. The picturesque Queen Anne Revival style was the height of fashion for Newport houses in the 1880s until the the arrival of the classically inspired, formally planned great mansions of the 1890s, such as neighboring Rosecliff (1902). Hatch Preparatory School purchased Ivy Tower in 1959. The school owned six Newport houses in the late 1950s at a time when these buildings were viewed as tax burdens. Today, the house is a private residence.

> "Everything in Newport is measured by the scale of millions. Even the flowers preach the gospel of wealth. Nature made it the most beautiful summer resort in the world; man has made it a monument to his colossal vanity. But it has the merit of being a beautiful and magnificent monument."

"Magnificent Newport," *Munsey's Magazine,* 1900

126 BELLEVUE AVENUE • NEWPORT

TOP: **Sherwood**
(photo 2006)

RIGHT: **Freidheim**
(c. 1885)

BOTTOM: **Loring Andrews House**
(c. 1875)

Sherwood
(1907)

Architect: George Champlin Mason
Remodeled by Francis L.V. Hoppin

Newport architect George Champlin Mason designed a Stick Style house in 1872 for Loring Andrews of New York, a self-made leather goods merchant and banker. Sugar refining magnate Theodore A. Havemeyer of New York acquired the house in 1880, renamed it Freidheim, and remodeled it in the Queen Anne Revival style. Pembroke and Sarah Jones of North Carolina bought Freidheim in 1906, renamed it Sherwood, and hired architect Francis Hoppin to remodel it in the Georgian Revival style. Noted for their lavish lifestyle, the Joneses hosted the engagement party for John F. Kennedy and Jacqueline Bouvier at Sherwood. The house became condominiums in 1971.

128 BELLEVUE AVENUE • NEWPORT

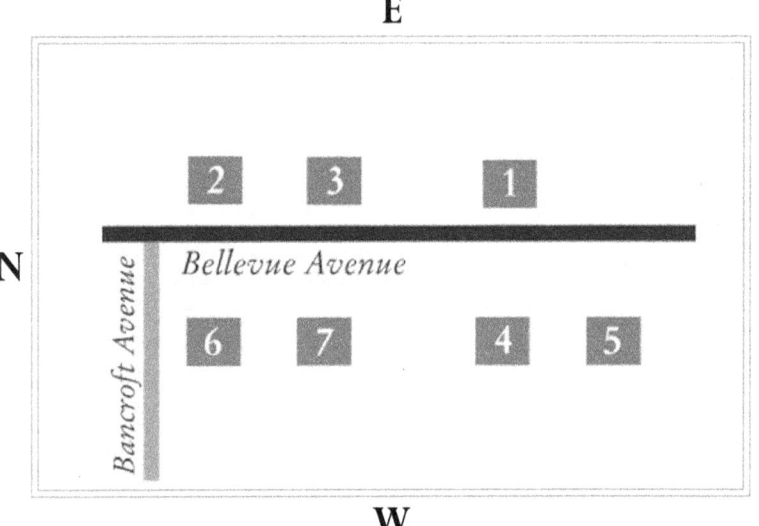

1. Marble House
2. Beechwood
3. Summer Wind
4. Laurelawn
5. Champ Soleil
6. Dromore

Marble House
& Its Neighbors

This block of Bellevue Avenue tells the story of social competitiveness and dominance by Newport's most glamorous residents, such as the Vanderbilts and Astors. A house on Bellevue Avenue was a symbol of social power during the Gilded Age, the years between 1865 and 1914 when America became the world's greatest financial and industrial power. There were over 300 summer residences in Newport at its height of popularity as a Gilded Age seaside resort. The rich, famous, and fashionable came to Newport to see and be seen, acting out their social pageant against the backdrop of great Bellevue Avenue houses. These houses have been celebrated as great works of architecture and as homes to famous families who shaped the nation's economic, social, and cultural life. They have also been criticized as examples of conspicuous consumption. Through historic preservation, Newport's historic houses, once thought relics of a bygone era, now attract over 800,000 visitors a year as museums that are time capsules of America's heritage.

> "The finest piece of architecture in Newport is the Marble House....This palace would shine like a jewel in any of the great capitals of Europe."
>
> "The Palace Cottages of Newport," *Munsey's Magazine,* c. 1893

Marble House

7
Marble House
(1888–1892)

Architect: Richard Morris Hunt

The opulent Marble House displayed the Vanderbilt family's social and financial preeminence and represented a new age of splendor in American building. Designed by Richard Morris Hunt, the house reportedly cost an estimated $11 million upon completion in 1892. Two landmarks of western architecture inspired Mrs. Vanderbilt's vision of Marble House: the Parthenon (fifth century B.C.), a temple to the goddess Athena in Athens, Greece; and the Petit Trianon (1764), a retreat in the form of a small temple for King Louis XV's mistress, Madame de Pompadour, in the gardens of Versailles. The grandeur of Marble House overshadowed the more modest neighboring Victorian cottage of Mrs. Vanderbilt's social rival, Mrs. William Backhouse Astor. Mr. and Mrs. Vanderbilt divorced in 1895. Later that year, the Vanderbilts' daughter, Consuelo, married the English 9th Duke of Marlborough in one of the most celebrated weddings of the Gilded Age. In 1912, Mrs. Vanderbilt commissioned the firm of Hunt & Hunt to design a Chinese Tea House on the grounds. In the early twentieth century, Mrs. Vanderbilt became an ardent champion of the women's right to vote movement. She hosted the "Conference of Great Women" for suffragists in the newly completed tea house in 1914. Today, the house is a property of The Preservation Society of Newport County.

Beechwood *(photo c. 1900)*

2
Beechwood
(1851–1852)

Architects: Calvert Vaux and Andrew Jackson Downing

The Italianate house called Beechwood became famous as the residence of the legendary Mrs. William Backhouse Astor, the leader of Gilded Age New York and Newport society. The term "the 400" referred to the socially acceptable received and entertained by Mrs. Astor. One of the richest families in America, the Astors commanded an immense fortune built on the fur trade and New York real estate. Calvert Vaux and Andrew Jackson Downing were leading designers of the midnineteenth century. Vaux designed the gates to New York's Central Park. Downing authored the best-selling book *The Architecture of Country Houses* (1852), which established the buildings and landscape features that comprised the ideal country estate. The 1970s subdivision of Beechwood resulted in the conversion of its greenhouses, stables, and coachman's house into separate private residences. The main house functioned as a museum until 2010. Today, the house is a private residence.

134 Bellevue Avenue • NEWPORT

Summer Wind *(photo c. 2004)*

3
Summer Wind
(1851–1852)

Architects: Calvert Vaux and Andrew Jackson Downing

This Italianate structure served as the gatehouse to the Beechwood estate before it was subdivided in the 1970s. Today it is a private residence.

> "And what should the villa be, architecturally?...The villa should indeed be a private house, where beauty, taste and moral culture are at home.... It is therefore in our villas that we must hope in this country to give the best and most complete manifestation of domestic architecture."
>
> A.J. Downing, *The Architecture of Country Houses,* 1850

Laurelawn *(photo 2004)*

4
Laurelawn
(1880)

Architects: Peabody and Stearns

Baltimore widow Frances Murdock hired the prominent Boston architects Peabody and Stearns to build this Stick Style cottage. The architects built many houses in Newport and the Berkshire resort town of Lenox, Massachusetts, known as the "inland Newport" due to its grand buildings and fashionable society. In 1882, Edward Padelford of Savannah, Georgia, purchased Laurelawn with his father's cotton fortune. The house has had several owners and remains a private residence.

Champ Soleil *(photo 2004)*

5
Champ Soleil (1929)

Architects: Polhemus and Coffin

Champ Soleil, or "sunny field," was built for Lucy Drexel Dahlgren, a descendant of the powerful Drexel banking family of Philadelphia. The house, modeled after eighteenth-century French manor houses, was one of the last grand houses to be built in Newport before the Great Depression of the 1930s curtailed such opulent construction. Robert Goelet IV purchased the house in 1948. The Goelets were a prominent New York family with a fortune in banking and real estate who built other great houses in Newport such as Ochre Court (1891). Today the house remains a private residence.

ABOVE: **Pelican** *(photo 2004)*
— *The Pelicans have since been removed.*

6
Dromore
(1984)

Architect: J.A. Griefendorf Designs

The land that is now the Dromore and Pelican Place properties remained open until the construction of these modern houses.

BELOW: **Dromore** *(photo 2004)*

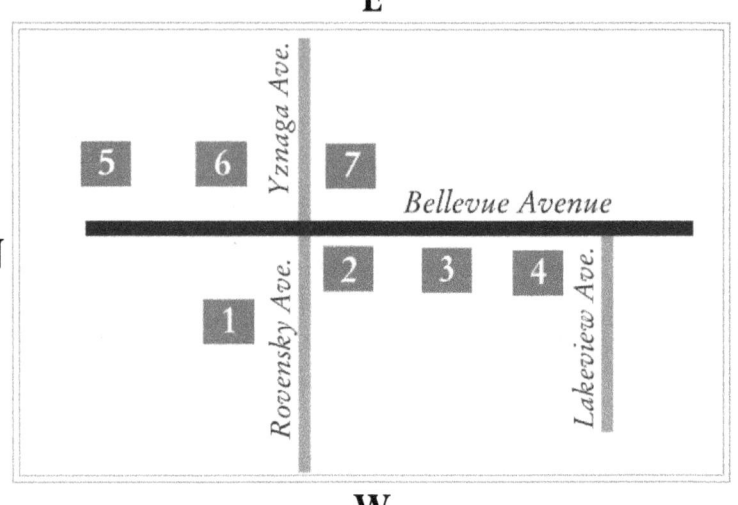

1. Rovensky Park
2. Weetamoe
3. Four Winds
4. The Beeches
5. Beaulieu
6. Clarendon Court
7. Miramar

Rovensky Park
& Its Neighbors

Endowed with spectacular natural scenery and a gentle climate, Newport was a gardener's paradise. This section of Bellevue Avenue reflects the rich horticultural heritage of the city and centuries of garden design, estate development, and land conservation. Beaulieu's extensive acreage was continually subdivided to make way for more summer cottages. The Widener family demolished three Victorian cottages to build the grand Miramar estate, famed for its formal French gardens. Today, Rovensky Park ensures the preservation of the area's historic character.

> **"The Island is exceedingly pleasant and healthful; and is celebrated for its fine women. Travelers, with propriety, call it the Eden of America."**
>
> Jedediah Morse writing on Newport and its environs, *The United States of America,* 1789

Rovensky Park *(photo 2011)*

[7] Rovensky Park (1960)

The only undeveloped space on Bellevue Avenue, Rovensky Park has never been the site of a building. Several prominent China Trade families with cottages on Bellevue Avenue owned parcels of the land that became Rovensky Park. Mae C. Rovensky was the wife of powerful New York banker and financier John E. Rovensky. In 1956, Mae C. Rovensky's will left a bequest to The Preservation Society of Newport County to acquire and maintain a park, creating what the bequest described as "breathing space for the city." Mrs. Rovensky's gift preserved the historic character of the district from further development.

> "There is very little land available for such public use within the city limits...and the trend has been to convert all spaces in some utilitarian purpose like housing."
>
> Robert Kerr, Director of The Preservation Society of Newport County, 1960

Weetamoe *(photo 2009)*

Weetamoe
(c. 1872)

Architects: Peabody and Stearns

Alfred Smith owned much of the farmland along Bellevue Avenue and promoted the area in the mid-nineteenth century as a fashionable summer resort. He subdivided lots and encouraged the cottage construction boom during the 1870s. He sold the site of Weetamoe to Hannah Swift, who hired the prominent Boston firm of Peabody and Stearns to build her Stick Style cottage. Nathaniel Thayer III, grandson of a noted Massachusetts clergyman, purchased the house in 1902. The Frazer family acquired the house in 1927 and eventually named it Catnip Cottage. The house remains a private residence.

Four Winds *(photo 2009)*

3
Four Winds
(c. 1871)

Architect: George Champlin Mason Sr.
Remodeled by Ogden Codman Jr. (1895)

George Champlin Mason Sr. built a Stick Style house in 1871 for Harriet Crowninshield. She was a member of a prominent family of successful merchants and political leaders descended from some of the first Massachusetts settlers in seventeenth-century Salem. Mason remodeled the house with Queen Anne Revival style additions in 1881 for Boston-based railroad investor Nathaniel Thayer Jr. In 1895, Thayer hired Ogden Codman Jr. to design a Classical Revival style addition to keep up with the latest fashions. The house remains a private residence.

150 BELLEVUE AVENUE • NEWPORT

The Beeches *(photo 1875)*

4
The Beeches
(c. 1870)

Architect: George Champlin Mason Sr.

George Champlin Mason Sr. designed this Second Empire style house for sugar merchant Moses Lazarus of New York. Lazarus's daughter Emma became a prolific writer and feminist. An excerpt from her sonnet *The New Colossus* (1883) is inscribed on the base of the Statue of Liberty: "Give me your tired, your poor, your huddled masses yearning to breathe free…" Moses supported Emma's writing both intellectually and financially. Transcendentalist writer Ralph Waldo Emerson also mentored and encouraged her. The Beeches remains a private residence.

> "They danced and they drove and they rode, they dined and wined and dressed and flirted and yachted and polo'd….on the old lawns and verandahs I saw them gather…and through the dusky old shrubberies came the light and sound of their feasts."
>
> Henry James, "The Sense of Newport," *The American Scene*, 1907

Beaulieu *(photo c. 1950)*

Beaulieu
(1856–1859)

Architect: Calvert Vaux

Peruvian ambassador Frederico Barreda built this Italianate style house in 1854. His estate also included about 15 acres now occupied by Clarendon Court (1904) and Miramar (1915). Architect Calvert Vaux, who also designed Beechwood on two lots to the north, was renowned for his work on New York's Central Park with Frederick Law Olmsted. Mr. and Mrs. William Waldorf Astor owned Beaulieu from the 1870s to 1901, when it was sold to Brigadier General Cornelius Vanderbilt III and his wife, Grace, a leading society hostess. The house remains a private residence.

> "Newport is more than a museum, that it is a museum where the pictures are alive and the figurines dance and talk. It is a fete, a regatta, a masked ball."
>
> Louis Auchincloss, introduction, *Newport Pleasures and Palaces* by Nancy Sirkis, 1963

ABOVE: **Clarendon Court** *(photo c. 1915)*
BELOW: **Monumental landscaping. Removing a hill at Clarendon Court to create a vista to the sea** *(photo c. 1970)*

6
Clarendon Court
(1903–1904)

Architect: Horace Trumbauer

Horace Trumbauer modeled this Georgian Revival style house after an eighteenth-century design by Colen Campbell. Clarendon Court was home to Edward Collins Knight Jr., son of a Philadelphia sugar refiner and director of the Pennsylania Railroad. Mae Cadwell Hawayd, who later married banker and financier John E. Rovensky, aquired the estate in 1930. The entrance gates to Clarendon Court were featured in the 1956 movie *High Society* starring Grace Kelly, Bing Crosby, and Frank Sinatra. Mr. and Mrs. Claus von Bülow owned Clarendon Court from 1970 to 1988. The house remains a private residence.

"Bellevue Avenue is the principal avenue in Newport…one sees a succession of beautiful villas and cottages on either hand, embowered in trees, shrubs, and flowering plants, and in full sight of the ocean–the lawns smoothly rolled and carefully cut."

George C. Mason, *Newport and Its Cottages,* 1875

156 BELLEVUE AVENUE • NEWPORT

ABOVE: **Aerial view of Miramar and its gardens** *(photo c. 1945)*
BELOW: **Miramar aerial** *(photo c. 1960)*

7
Miramar
(1912–1915)

Architect: Horace Trumbauer

George Widener, a Philadelphia transportation magnate, commissioned Horace Trumbauer to design the Classical Revival style Miramar, one of the most splendid Gilded Age cottages. Although he had no formal training in architecture, Trumbauer designed The Elms (1901), Chetwode (1903), and Clarendon Court (1904) on Bellevue Avenue. Mr. Widener and his son Harry died on the *Titanic* in 1912. George's widow, Eleanor Elkins Widener, completed Miramar. She also funded Harvard University's Harry Elkins Widener Memorial Library in her son's memory. Mrs. Widener married Dr. Alexander Hamilton Rice in 1915. They entertained frequently at Miramar until her death in 1937. Upon Dr. Rice's death in 1957, Miramar passed to the Rhode Island Episcopal Diocese and later to a girls' school. Today, Miramar is a private residence. The house and grounds are undergoing extensive conservation.

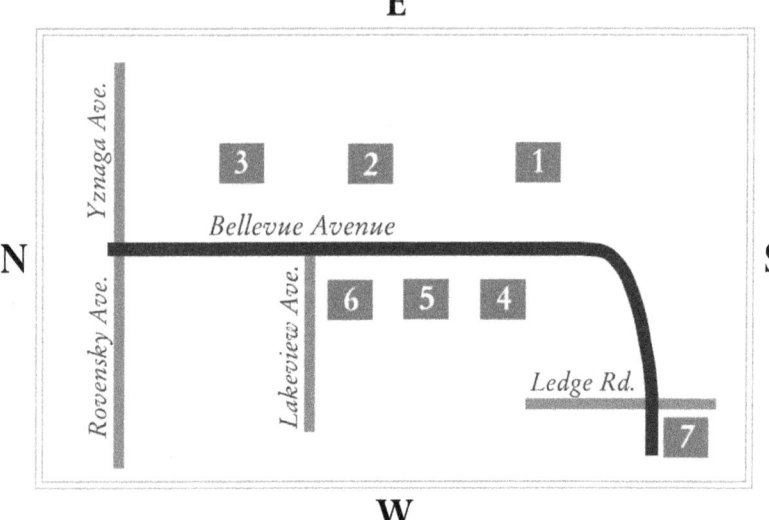

1. Rough Point
2. Roselawn
3. Rock Cliff
4. Ocean View
5. Belcourt
6. Resthaven
7. Quatrel

Rough Point
& Its Neighbors

This part of Bellevue Avenue reflects the architectural variety of nineteenth-century Newport houses, from the Gothic Revival and Second Empire villas of the early 1850s to the Stick Style cottages of the 1870s and the Beaux Arts mansions of the 1880s and 1890s. Many of these houses were continually remodeled in order to keep up with changing architectural tastes in a summer resort renowned as a center of fashionable life. Today, these buildings survive as examples of architectural innovation by the nation's leading designers.

"Newport, rich in the historical monuments of three centuries, must bend every effort to serve the purpose of cultural memory. And, in the intelligent appraisal of her architectural monuments, she must not lose sight of those cultural essentials of new invention and dynamic growth which are embodied in much of her nineteenth century architecture."

Vincent J. Scully Jr. and Antoinette Downing,
The Architectural Heritage of Newport, RI, 1967

160 BELLEVUE AVENUE • NEWPORT

Rough Point *(photo 1922)*

Rough Point
(1888–1891)

Architects: Peabody and Stearns
Renovations by Horace Trumbauer

Rough Point was designed for Frederick William Vanderbilt, brother of William K., who built Marble House (1892), and Cornelius, who built The Breakers (1895), in Newport. The firm of Olmsted Brothers designed the grounds. William B. Leeds, known as the "tin plate king," purchased the house in 1907. Tobacco and energy magnate James B. Duke acquired the house in 1922 and engaged architect Horace Trumbauer to remodel the building. James Duke's only child and heir, Doris, maintained the house until her death in 1993. Acclaimed as one of the richest women in America, Doris Duke became a noted collector, philanthropist, and preservationist, founding the Newport Restoration Foundation in 1968. The foundation has restored more than eighty eighteenth-century buildings in Newport, contributing to the preservation of the city's historic core. Today Rough Point is a museum open to the public.

Roselawn *(photo 2008)*

2
Roselawn
(1852–1853)

Architect: William A. Sweet
Remodeled by George Champlin Mason Sr.

Aware of Newport's potential as a fashionable summer resort, real estate speculator William Sweet began construction of the Gothic Revival style Roselawn on the recently completed Bellevue Avenue in 1852. Abraham Peckham completed the building and sold it to James T. Rhodes of Providence in 1853, including rights to use Bailey's Beach with a bathing car, a portable beach cabana, and to gather seaweed. Mr. Rhodes's descendants lived at Roselawn for 111 years. Mr. Rhodes's granddaughter, Mrs. George H. Hull, was a member of "the 400," the name given to New York society's most prominent inner circle. Mrs. Hull died in 1964 at ninety-three, and the house passed through several owners. Today the house remains a private residence.

TOP: **Rock Cliff** *(photo c. 1880)*
BOTTOM: **Rock Cliff** *(photo c. 1940)*

3
Rock Cliff
(c. 1869)

Architect: George Champlin Mason Sr.
Remodeled by George Champlin Mason Jr.

Rock Cliff began as a Stick Style cottage and through subsequent remodeling became a Classical Revival villa. The move from mid-Victorian picturesque wooden styles to classically inspired stone houses in the early 1900s was typical in Newport as tastes evolved. Rock Cliff was home to many prominent members of Newport's summer colony, such as the Cushings, Drexels, and Vanderbilts.

> "White elephants...all house and no garden...What an idea...to have seen this miniature spot of earth...as a mere breeding ground for white elephants...their averted owners, roused from a witless dream, wonder what in the world is to be done with them. The answer...can only be... to let them stand there always, vast and blank, for reminder to those concerned with the prohibited degrees of witlessness, and of the peculiarly awkward vengeances of affronted proportion and discretion."
>
> Henry James, "The Sense of Newport," *The American Scene*, 1907

Ocean View *(photo 2009)*

4
Ocean View
(c. 1866, Rebuilt in 1985)

Architect: William Russell Walker

Ocean View is in the Second Empire style, the height of fashion for Newport cottages in the 1860s. Ogden Mills inherited from his father, Darien, who established the family fortune from banking and railroads associated with the silver and gold mines of Nevada and California. The Mills' son, Ogden Livingston Mills, served as Secretary of the Treasury under President Herbert Hoover. Ocean View was rebuilt in 1985 and remains a private residence.

> "He went to Newport and tried to be fashionable…. Newport was charming, but it asked for no education and gave none….Society seemed founded on the law that all was for the best New Yorkers in the best of Newports, and that all young people were rich if they could waltz."
>
> Henry Adams, *The Education of Henry Adams*, 1905

Belcourt *(photo c. 1890)*

5
Belcourt
(1891–1894)

Architect: Richard Morris Hunt

Oliver Hazard Perry Belmont hired Richard Morris Hunt to design a summer villa inspired by a Louis XIII period hunting lodge. A well-known horseman, Belmont gave over one wing of the first floor of his house to luxurious stables. O.H.P. Belmont's father, August Belmont, was the Rothschild banking agent in America. His mother, born Caroline Slidell Perry of Newport, was the daughter of Commodore Matthew Perry, famed for opening Japan to western trade in the 1850s. O.H.P. Belmont married Alva Vanderbilt in 1896 after her divorce from William K. Vanderbilt. Alva closed her Bellevue Avenue cottage, Marble House (1892), and came to live at Belcourt. Renowned as the "dean of American architecture," Hunt was the first American to study at the prestigious École des Beaux Arts in Paris. Belcourt is one of the earliest classically inspired palatial villas in Newport, which were built in great number during the period 1890 to 1914 and changed the face of the city from picturesque wooden houses to palatial stone mansions. Today, Belcourt is privately owned.

Resthaven *(photo 2009)*

6
Resthaven
(1869–1870)

Architect: Richard Morris Hunt

Prominent China Trade merchant and financier John N.A. Griswold owned several properties on Bellevue Avenue as investments. He commissioned Richard Morris Hunt to build this Stick Style villa, which he sold, fully furnished, upon its completion to the New York widow Anna Gilbert. Anna Gilbert's son, Charles Pierrepont Gilbert, was a New York architect who trained at the École des Beaux Arts in Paris. He and his wife, Clara, summered at Resthaven until 1916. The house remains a private residence.

> "Hunt's greatest successes were in his residences. No other form of building was so congenial to him... Skilled in every phase of his art, an architect whose work varied from business buildings to memorial monuments, from great public buildings to private houses, it is in the last that his genius found its ripest expression. It is by his houses he will be judged."
>
> Barr Ferree, "Richard Morris Hunt: His Art and Work," *Architecture and Building*, December 7, 1895

TOP: **Quatrel** *(photo 2006)*
BOTTOM: **Fairbourne** *(photo c. 1875)*

7
Quatrel (Fairbourne) (1853–1854)

Architect: Thomas Tefft
Remodeled by Ogden Codman Jr. (1900)

Built for the banker Earl Mason, the house was originally known as Fairbourne. Both Mason and the architect Thomas Tefft were from Providence. A founding member of the American Institute of Architects in 1857, Tefft knew the leading architectural and design theorists of his era, such as John Ruskin, Charles Barry, and Owen Jones. He died of a fever in Florence, Italy, at age thirty-three. New York lawyer and art connoisseur Egerton Winthrop owned Fairbourne from 1880 to 1926. He hired Ogden Codman Jr. to remodel the picturesque Victorian cottage in the Classical Revival style in 1900. Winthrop was a close friend of his neighbor, the writer Edith Wharton. He advised Wharton on artistic and literary subjects that greatly influenced her development as a writer. Louis and Elaine Lorillard named the house Quatrel, summering there from 1950 to 1961. The Lorillard family created the Lorillard Tobacco Company. Later generations founded Tuxedo Park, New York. Today Quatrel is a private residence.

Afterword
Ronald Lee Fleming, FAICP
The Bellevue Avenue Markers and Stories of Historic Preservation

*H*istoric markers can't completely capture the mythos of a street as famous as Bellevue Avenue; they are a modest intervention of encapsulated memories in the streetscape. Captions and photographs do pay tribute block by block. They recover some of the drama behind hedges, fences, and walls and describe most of the buildings along the street. This in itself was an innovation; learning about the entire street rather than just selected landmarks. Caring about the whole as the sum of its parts is a more comprehensive approach that conversely supports an incremental perception of place. Each block has a marker that the individual encounters as he or she makes the gentle perambulation of this walking tour.

The markers conjure up the story of aspirant America. Two miles of houses marking the ambitions, pretensions, and stolid verities of both established wealth and a newly enriched capitalistic class. Many of these villas were built by hard-fisted men without a college education. They were titans of industry and commerce before the invention of business school. But to paraphrase one early twentieth-century observer, behind almost every facade there were also tales of sorrow, loneliness, or alienation. Newport society was a matriarchy; the men were largely absent, as social historians often noted. But our markers don't look that deeply on the human condition; our markers are about the history of preservation. Though there is plenty of gossip buried between lines, our primary mission was to build an awareness of the physical fabric of the street in order to better protect and conserve it.

We recognized that our preservation mission was broader than the houses The Preservation Society of Newport County owned. There is now a National Historic Landmark District with a local historical commission reviewing changes to buildings. This was done in response to demolitions in the early 1960s, including the tragic loss of Villa Rosa, the Ogden Codman Jr. masterpiece next to The Elms, which went down with its chandeliers still swinging. It was the victim of out-of-town speculators. Behind most preservation stories there is this specter of loss, and, as the markers note, the battle for The Elms in the early 1960s was the turning point of consciousness-raising.

That consciousness-raising goes on today. At this writing the avenue isn't entirely secure. Gates and fences can still be removed with the granting of a city permit that does not require Historic District Commission review. Brick entrance gates have been demolished or altered in several locations, replaced with mediocre modern designs. A modest loss, one can argue, but the incremental loss of character still threatens the street. Efforts to add protection for gates and fences to the Historic District ordinance failed on a tie vote at the city council in 2010 despite community support. National Historic Landmark Districts in other nationally ranked coastal cities like Annapolis and Charleston, also candidates for World Heritage designation along with Newport, have this protection. Indeed, I have contemplated tearing down a piece of my own crumbling wall on Bellevue Avenue and replacing it with chain link fence, just to prove the point. Sometimes the shock of an alternative can be useful.

But there remains more to do in the interpretation of the

avenue. Nearby streets could feature historic markers, continuing this remarkable and walkable heritage trail. The markers encourage us to dismount and to notice the tactile details of the street, the bits of forged iron and carved limestone, the gates of the great houses and their vases with grotesque heads, such as those at The Elms; to read the caption on the statue of Gilded Age financier August Belmont in front of the Preservation Society's headquarters; and to notice that the cast iron owls with blinking electric eyes that startled passersby are no longer on a fence at Stone Villa, demolished in the 1950s for a shopping center.

The markers help us to look more closely at this place and to look longer. Each of these elements can release a mental sensation as the German word for monument, *denkmal*, literally connotes "time pause." By bringing the narrative to the streetscape, we can hope that the citizens will eventually take a longer view and recognize that the Bellevue Avenue Historic District, built for the pleasure of a few, now is the golden goose that keeps visitors coming, and coming back, to Newport.

www.ingramcontent.com/pod-product-compliance
Lightning Source LLC
LaVergne TN
LVHW011419080426
835512LV00005B/158